SLOW COOKER COOKBOOK FOR LABRADOR RETRIEVERS

60 Homemade and Healthy Recipes for Your Furry Friend

Jeffrey D. Mike

Contents

INTRODUCTION

Bailey, an energetic Labrador Retriever whose boundless enthusiasm brightens every day for her loving family. Despite their hectic schedules, they're committed to giving Bailey the best care possible.

They stumbled upon a treasure which is this Slow Cooker Cookbook designed specifically for Labrador Retrievers like Bailey.

It is not just a book of recipes; it was a game-changer that made mealtime a joy for both Bailey and her family.

From delectable Chicken and Sweet Potato Stew to tantalizing Salmon and Quinoa Delight, each dish was carefully crafted to provide Bailey with a balanced, nutritious diet.

The convenience of this slow cooker made it a breeze for Bailey's family to whip up these meals, filling their home with delicious aromas.

As Bailey savored every bite, her health thrived, her coat shone, and her playful spirit soared.

This Slow Cooker Cookbook became a symbol of love and dedication to Bailey's well-being, turning ordinary meals into moments of joy and nourishment.

Join us on Bailey's culinary adventure, where every meal is a celebration of health, happiness, and the special bond we share with our furry companions.

RECIPES

Chicken and Sweet Potato Stew

Serves: 4

Ingredients:

- Chicken breast (1 lb, boneless and skinless)

- Sweet potatoes (2, peeled and diced)

- Carrots (1 cup, sliced)

- Celery (1 cup, sliced)

- Low-sodium chicken broth (2 cups)

- Onion (1, diced)

- Garlic (2 cloves, minced)

- Thyme (1 tsp, dried)

- Salt and pepper to taste

Preparation:

- Place chicken, sweet potatoes, carrots, celery, onion, garlic, thyme, salt, and pepper in the slow cooker.
- Pour chicken broth over the ingredients.
- Cook on low for 6-8 hours or high for 3-4 hours until chicken is tender and vegetables are cooked.
- Shred the chicken before serving.

Nutritional values per serving:

- Protein: 25g
- Fat: 5g
- Carbohydrates: 30g
- Calories: 250

Serves: 3

Ingredients:

- Ground turkey (1 lb)

- Pumpkin puree (1 cup)

- Rolled oats (1 cup)

- Low-sodium chicken broth (2 cups)

- Apple (1, diced)

- Cinnamon (1 tsp)

- Honey (2 tbsp)

- Salt to taste

Preparation:

- Brown ground turkey in a pan, then transfer to the slow cooker.

- Add pumpkin puree, rolled oats, chicken broth, apple, cinnamon, honey, and salt.

- Stir well and cook on low for 4-5 hours until oats are tender.

- Adjust sweetness with additional honey if desired.

Nutritional values per serving:

- Protein: 20g

- Fat: 8g

- Carbohydrates: 40g

- Calories: 300

Serves: 4

Ingredients:

- Stewing beef (1 lb, cubed)
- Potatoes (2, diced)
- Spinach (2 cups)
- Onion (1, diced)
- Garlic (2 cloves, minced)
- Paprika (1 tsp)
- Salt and pepper to taste

Preparation:

- Brown stewing beef in a pan, then transfer to the slow cooker.
- Add potatoes, spinach, onion, garlic, paprika, salt, and pepper.

- Cook on low for 6-8 hours or high for 3-4 hours until beef is tender and potatoes are cooked.
- Mash lightly for a hash-like consistency before serving.

Nutritional values per serving:

- Protein: 30g
- Fat: 10g
- Carbohydrates: 25g
- Calories: 300

Serves: 3

Ingredients:

- Salmon fillets (3, skinless)
- Quinoa (1 cup, cooked)
- Broccoli florets (1 cup)
- Cherry tomatoes (1 cup, halved)
- Lemon juice (2 tbsp)
- Olive oil (2 tbsp)
- Dill (1 tsp, dried)
- Salt and pepper to taste

Preparation:

- Season salmon fillets with lemon juice, olive oil, dill, salt, and pepper.
- Place salmon in the slow cooker.

- In a bowl, mix cooked quinoa, broccoli, and cherry tomatoes.

- Spread the quinoa mixture around the salmon.

- Cook on low for 2-3 hours until salmon is cooked through and vegetables are tender.

Nutritional values per serving:

- Protein: 25g

- Fat: 12g

- Carbohydrates: 20g

- Calories: 280

Serves: 6

Ingredients:

- Eggs (8)
- Milk (1 cup)
- Cheddar cheese (1 cup, shredded)
- Spinach (2 cups, chopped)
- Bell peppers (1, diced)
- Onion (1, diced)
- Garlic (2 cloves, minced)
- Salt and pepper to taste

Preparation:

- In a bowl, beat eggs with milk, salt, and pepper.
- Grease the slow cooker and layer spinach, bell peppers, onion, garlic, and cheese.

- Pour the egg mixture over the layers.
- Cook on low for 3-4 hours until set.

Nutritional values per serving:

- Protein: 15g
- Fat: 12g
- Carbohydrates: 8g
- Calories: 180

Serves: 4

Ingredients:

- Turkey sausage (1 lb, sliced)
- Potatoes (2, diced)
- Eggs (4)
- Bell peppers (1, diced)
- Onion (1, diced)
- Garlic (2 cloves, minced)
- Olive oil (2 tbsp)
- Salt and pepper to taste

Preparation:

- Brown turkey sausage in a pan with olive oil, then transfer to the slow cooker.

- Add potatoes, bell peppers, onion, garlic, salt, and pepper.

- Cook on low for 4-5 hours until potatoes are tender.

- Scramble eggs separately and serve over the sausage and potato mixture.

Nutritional values per serving:

- Protein: 20g

- Fat: 10g

- Carbohydrates: 15g

- Calories: 220

Serves: 4

Ingredients:

- Lamb leg meat (1 lb, cubed)

- White rice (1 cup, uncooked)

- Carrots (1 cup, sliced)

- Peas (1 cup)

- Onion (1, diced)

- Garlic (2 cloves, minced)

- Rosemary (1 tsp, dried)

- Salt and pepper to taste

Preparation:

- Brown lamb meat in a pan, then transfer to the slow cooker.

- Add white rice, carrots, peas, onion, garlic, rosemary, salt, and pepper.

- Pour enough water or broth to cover the ingredients.

- Cook on low for 6-8 hours or high for 3-4 hours until lamb is tender and rice is cooked.

Nutritional values per serving:

- Protein: 30g

- Fat: 12g

- Carbohydrates: 35g

- Calories: 320

Serves: 4

Ingredients:

- Pork loin (1 lb, cubed)

- Rolled oats (1 cup)

- Apple (1, diced)

- Low-sodium chicken broth (2 cups)

- Cinnamon (1 tsp)

- Honey (2 tbsp)

- Salt to taste

Preparation:

- Brown pork loin cubes in a pan, then transfer to the slow cooker.

- Add rolled oats, diced apple, chicken broth, cinnamon, honey, and salt.
- Stir well and cook on low for 4-5 hours until oats are tender.
- Adjust sweetness with additional honey if desired.

Nutritional values per serving:

- Protein: 25g
- Fat: 8g
- Carbohydrates: 40g
- Calories: 300

Serves: 6

Ingredients:

- Chicken thighs (1 lb, boneless and skinless)

- Broccoli florets (3 cups)

- Brown rice (1 cup, uncooked)

- Low-sodium chicken broth (2 cups)

- Onion (1, diced)

- Garlic (2 cloves, minced)

- Paprika (1 tsp)

- Cheddar cheese (1 cup, shredded)

- Salt and pepper to taste

Preparation:

- Brown chicken thighs in a pan, then transfer to the slow cooker.

- Add broccoli florets, brown rice, chicken broth, onion, garlic, paprika, salt, and pepper.

- Stir well and cook on low for 6-8 hours or high for 3-4 hours until chicken is cooked through and rice is tender.

- Sprinkle shredded cheddar cheese over the casserole before serving.

Nutritional values per serving:

- Protein: 30g

- Fat: 15g

- Carbohydrates: 30g

- Calories: 350

Serves: 4

Ingredients:

- Turkey bacon (1/2 lb, chopped)

- Potatoes (2, diced)

- Carrots (1 cup, sliced)

- Celery (1 cup, sliced)

- Low-sodium chicken broth (4 cups)

- Onion (1, diced)

- Garlic (2 cloves, minced)

- Thyme (1 tsp, dried)

- Salt and pepper to taste

Preparation:

- Cook turkey bacon in a pan until crispy, then transfer to the slow cooker.

- Add potatoes, carrots, celery, chicken broth, onion, garlic, thyme, salt, and pepper.
- Cook on low for 6-8 hours or high for 3-4 hours until vegetables are tender.
- Adjust seasoning if needed before serving.

Nutritional values per serving:

- Protein: 15g
- Fat: 8g
- Carbohydrates: 20g
- Calories: 200

Serves: 4

Ingredients:

- Stewing beef (1 lb, cubed)

- Pumpkin puree (1 cup)

- Potatoes (2, diced)

- Carrots (1 cup, sliced)

- Low-sodium beef broth (2 cups)

- Onion (1, diced)

- Garlic (2 cloves, minced)

- Rosemary (1 tsp, dried)

- Salt and pepper to taste

Preparation:

- Brown stewing beef in a pan, then transfer to the slow cooker.

- Add pumpkin puree, potatoes, carrots, beef broth, onion, garlic, rosemary, salt, and pepper.

- Cook on low for 6-8 hours or high for 3-4 hours until beef is tender and vegetables are cooked.

- Mash some of the pumpkin and potatoes to thicken the stew if desired.

Nutritional values per serving:

- Protein: 30g

- Fat: 10g

- Carbohydrates: 25g

- Calories: 300

Serves: 3

Ingredients:

- Salmon fillets (3, skinless)
- Potatoes (2, diced)
- Carrots (1 cup, sliced)
- Celery (1 cup, sliced)
- Low-sodium chicken broth (2 cups)
- Milk (1 cup)
- Onion (1, diced)
- Garlic (2 cloves, minced)
- Dill (1 tsp, dried)
- Salt and pepper to taste

Preparation:

- Place salmon fillets in the slow cooker.

- Add potatoes, carrots, celery, chicken broth, milk, onion, garlic, dill, salt, and pepper.
- Cook on low for 2-3 hours until salmon flakes easily and vegetables are tender.
- Stir in milk and dill just before serving.

Nutritional values per serving:

- Protein: 25g
- Fat: 8g
- Carbohydrates: 20g
- Calories: 260

Serves: 4

Ingredients:

- Eggs (8)

- Whole wheat tortillas (4)

- Cheddar cheese (1 cup, shredded)

- Turkey sausage (1/2 lb, cooked and crumbled)

- Spinach (2 cups)

- Bell peppers (1, diced)

- Onion (1, diced)

- Garlic (2 cloves, minced)

- Olive oil (2 tbsp)

- Salt and pepper to taste

Preparation:

- In a pan, sauté turkey sausage, spinach, bell peppers, onion, and garlic with olive oil until vegetables are tender.

- Scramble eggs in the same pan until cooked.

- Warm tortillas and assemble burritos with scrambled eggs, vegetable-sausage mixture, and shredded cheese.

- Roll up and serve warm.

Nutritional values per serving:

- Protein: 20g

- Fat: 10g

- Carbohydrates: 30g

- Calories: 280

Serves: 4

Ingredients:

- Bell peppers (4, halved and seeds removed)

- Ground turkey (1 lb)

- Quinoa (1 cup, cooked)

- Tomato sauce (1 cup)

- Onion (1, diced)

- Garlic (2 cloves, minced)

- Italian seasoning (1 tbsp)

- Olive oil (2 tbsp)

- Salt and pepper to taste

Preparation:

- Precook bell peppers in boiling water for 5 minutes, then drain and set aside.

- In a pan, cook ground turkey with olive oil, onion, garlic, Italian seasoning, salt, and pepper until browned.

- Stir in cooked quinoa and tomato sauce.

- Stuff the bell pepper halves with the turkey-quinoa mixture.

- Place stuffed peppers in the slow cooker, add a little water at the bottom, and cook on low for 3-4 hours.

Nutritional values per serving:

- Protein: 25g

- Fat: 10g

- Carbohydrates: 30g

- Calories: 280

Chicken and Rice Congee

Serves: 4

Ingredients:

- Chicken thighs (1 lb, boneless and skinless)
- White rice (1 cup, uncooked)
- Ginger (1 tbsp, minced)
- Low-sodium chicken broth (4 cups)
- Green onions (2, chopped)
- Salt and pepper to taste

Preparation:

- Place chicken thighs, white rice, ginger, chicken broth, salt, and pepper in the slow cooker.
- Cook on low for 6-8 hours or high for 3-4 hours until chicken is tender and rice is soft.
- Shred the chicken and stir well to combine.

- Garnish with chopped green onions before serving.

Nutritional values per serving:

- Protein: 30g
- Fat: 8g
- Carbohydrates: 30g
- Calories: 320

Serves: 4

Ingredients:

- Stewing beef (1 lb, cubed)
- Barley (1/2 cup, uncooked)
- Carrots (1 cup, sliced)
- Celery (1 cup, sliced)
- Low-sodium beef broth (4 cups)
- Onion (1, diced)
- Garlic (2 cloves, minced)
- Thyme (1 tsp, dried)
- Salt and pepper to taste

Preparation:

- Brown stewing beef in a pan, then transfer to the slow cooker.

- Add barley, carrots, celery, beef broth, onion, garlic, thyme, salt, and pepper.
- Cook on low for 6-8 hours or high for 3-4 hours until beef is tender and barley is cooked.
- Adjust seasoning if needed before serving.

Nutritional values per serving:

- Protein: 25g
- Fat: 10g
- Carbohydrates: 30g
- Calories: 300

Serves: 4

Ingredients:

- Ground turkey (1 lb)

- Sweet potatoes (2, peeled and diced)

- Bell peppers (1, diced)

- Onion (1, diced)

- Garlic (2 cloves, minced)

- Olive oil (2 tbsp)

- Paprika (1 tsp)

- Salt and pepper to taste

Preparation:

- In a pan, cook ground turkey with olive oil, onion, garlic, paprika, salt, and pepper until browned.

- Transfer cooked turkey mixture to the slow cooker.

- Add diced sweet potatoes and bell peppers.

- Cook on low for 4-5 hours until sweet potatoes are tender.

Nutritional values per serving:

- Protein: 20g

- Fat: 8g

- Carbohydrates: 25g

- Calories: 230

Serves: 4

Ingredients:

- Salmon fillets (2, skinless)
- Eggs (8)
- Milk (1/2 cup)
- Peas (1 cup)
- Cheddar cheese (1/2 cup, shredded)
- Onion (1, diced)
- Garlic (2 cloves, minced)
- Olive oil (2 tbsp)
- Salt and pepper to taste

Preparation:

- In a pan, cook salmon fillets with olive oil until cooked through, then flake into pieces.

- In the same pan, sauté onion and garlic until softened.

- In a bowl, beat eggs with milk, salt, and pepper.

- Grease the slow cooker and layer cooked salmon, onion-garlic mixture, peas, and shredded cheese.

- Pour the egg mixture over the layers.

- Cook on low for 3-4 hours until set and golden on top.

Nutritional values per serving:

- Protein: 25g

- Fat: 12g

- Carbohydrates: 15g

- Calories: 260

Serves: 4

Ingredients:

- Chicken thighs (1 lb, boneless and skinless)
- Lentils (1 cup, rinsed)
- Carrots (1 cup, sliced)
- Celery (1 cup, sliced)
- Low-sodium chicken broth (3 cups)
- Onion (1, diced)
- Garlic (2 cloves, minced)
- Cumin (1 tsp, ground)
- Paprika (1 tsp)
- Salt and pepper to taste

Preparation:

- Place chicken thighs, lentils, carrots, celery, chicken broth, onion, garlic, cumin, paprika, salt, and pepper in the slow cooker.
- Cook on low for 6-8 hours or high for 3-4 hours until chicken is tender and lentils are cooked.
- Shred the chicken before serving.

Nutritional values per serving:

- Protein: 30g
- Fat: 5g
- Carbohydrates: 35g
- Calories: 280

Serves: 6

Ingredients:

- Ground turkey (1 lb)
- Pumpkin puree (1 cup)
- Whole wheat bread (4 slices, cubed)
- Eggs (6)
- Milk (1 cup)
- Sage (1 tsp, dried)
- Salt and pepper to taste

Preparation:

- Brown ground turkey in a pan, then drain excess fat.
- In a bowl, mix pumpkin puree, cubed whole wheat bread, eggs, milk, sage, salt, and pepper.

- Grease the slow cooker and pour in the pumpkin-bread mixture.
- Top with cooked ground turkey.
- Cook on low for 4-5 hours until set and golden on top.

Nutritional values per serving:

- Protein: 20g
- Fat: 8g
- Carbohydrates: 25g
- Calories: 240

LUNCH

Serves: 4

Ingredients:

- Chicken breast (1 lb, boneless and skinless)
- Brown rice (1 cup, uncooked)
- Carrots (2, diced)
- Celery (2 stalks, diced)
- Low-sodium chicken broth (4 cups)
- Onion (1, diced)
- Garlic (2 cloves, minced)
- Salt and pepper to taste

Preparation:

- Place chicken, rice, carrots, celery, onion, garlic, and chicken broth in the slow cooker.
- Cook on low for 6-8 hours or high for 3-4 hours until chicken is cooked through and rice is tender.
- Shred the chicken before serving and adjust seasoning if needed.

Nutritional values per serving:

- Protein: 25g
- Fat: 5g
- Carbohydrates: 30g
- Calories: 250

Serves: 3

Ingredients:

- Ground turkey (1 lb)

- Sweet potatoes (2, peeled and diced)

- Low-sodium chicken broth (2 cups)

- Green beans (1 cup, trimmed and chopped)

- Onion (1, diced)

- Garlic (2 cloves, minced)

- Sage (1 tsp, dried)

- Salt and pepper to taste

Preparation:

- Brown ground turkey in a pan, then transfer to the slow cooker.

- Add sweet potatoes, chicken broth, green beans, onion, garlic, sage, salt, and pepper.
- Cook on low for 4-5 hours until sweet potatoes are tender.

Nutritional values per serving:

- Protein: 20g
- Fat: 8g
- Carbohydrates: 25g
- Calories: 230

Serves: 4

Ingredients:

- Stewing beef (1 lb, cubed)

- Potatoes (2, diced)

- Carrots (1 cup, sliced)

- Green beans (1 cup, trimmed and chopped)

- Low-sodium beef broth (2 cups)

- Onion (1, diced)

- Garlic (2 cloves, minced)

- Thyme (1 tsp, dried)

- Salt and pepper to taste

Preparation:

- Brown beef in a pan, then transfer to the slow cooker.

- Add potatoes, carrots, green beans, beef broth, onion, garlic, thyme, salt, and pepper.
- Cook on low for 6-8 hours or high for 3-4 hours until beef is tender.

Nutritional values per serving:

- Protein: 30g
- Fat: 10g
- Carbohydrates: 20g
- Calories: 280

Serves: 3

Ingredients:

- Salmon fillets (3, skinless)

- Quinoa (1 cup, cooked)

- Cucumber (1, diced)

- Cherry tomatoes (1 cup, halved)

- Red onion (1/2, thinly sliced)

- Lemon juice (2 tbsp)

- Olive oil (2 tbsp)

- Dill (1 tsp, dried)

- Salt and pepper to taste

Preparation:

- Season salmon with salt, pepper, and dill. Place in the slow cooker.

- In a bowl, combine cooked quinoa, cucumber, tomatoes, red onion, lemon juice, olive oil, salt, and pepper.
- Serve the salmon over the quinoa salad.

Nutritional values per serving:

- Protein: 25g
- Fat: 12g
- Carbohydrates: 25g
- Calories: 300

Serves: 6

Ingredients:

- Eggs (8)
- Milk (1 cup)
- Cheddar cheese (1 cup, shredded)
- Spinach (2 cups, chopped)
- Red bell pepper (1, diced)
- Onion (1, diced)
- Garlic (2 cloves, minced)
- Salt and pepper to taste

Preparation:

- In a bowl, whisk together eggs, milk, salt, and pepper.

- Grease the slow cooker and layer spinach, bell pepper, onion, garlic, and cheese.
- Pour the egg mixture over the layers.
- Cook on low for 3-4 hours until set.

Nutritional values per serving:

- Protein: 15g
- Fat: 10g
- Carbohydrates: 8g
- Calories: 180

Serves: 4

Ingredients:

- Lamb leg meat (1 lb, cubed)

- Brown rice (1 cup, uncooked)

- Chicken broth (2 cups)

- Carrots (1 cup, diced)

- Peas (1 cup)

- Onion (1, diced)

- Garlic (2 cloves, minced)

- Cumin (1 tsp, ground)

- Salt and pepper to taste

Preparation:

- Brown lamb in a pan, then transfer to the slow cooker.

- Add brown rice, chicken broth, carrots, peas, onion, garlic, cumin, salt, and pepper.
- Cook on low for 6-8 hours or high for 3-4 hours until lamb is tender and rice is cooked.

Nutritional values per serving:

- Protein: 28g
- Fat: 12g
- Carbohydrates: 35g
- Calories: 320

Serves: 4

Ingredients:

- Pork loin (1 lb, cubed)

- Apples (2, peeled and diced)

- Potatoes (2, diced)

- Low-sodium chicken broth (2 cups)

- Onion (1, diced)

- Garlic (2 cloves, minced)

- Sage (1 tsp, dried)

- Salt and pepper to taste

Preparation:

- Brown pork in a pan, then transfer to the slow cooker.

- Add apples, potatoes, chicken broth, onion, garlic, sage, salt, and pepper.

- Cook on low for 6-8 hours or high for 3-4 hours until pork is tender.

Nutritional values per serving:

- Protein: 22g

- Fat: 8g

- Carbohydrates: 26g

- Calories: 280

Serves: 4

Ingredients:

- Chicken thighs (1 lb, boneless and skinless, diced)
- Lentils (1 cup, rinsed)
- Coconut milk (1 can)
- Onion (1, diced)
- Garlic (2 cloves, minced)
- Ginger (1 tbsp, minced)
- Curry powder (2 tbsp)
- Salt and pepper to taste

Preparation:

- Combine all ingredients in the slow cooker.

- Cook on low for 6-8 hours or high for 3-4 hours until chicken is cooked through and lentils are tender.

Nutritional values per serving:

- Protein: 30g
- Fat: 15g
- Carbohydrates: 20g
- Calories: 320

Serves: 6

Ingredients:

- Ground turkey (1 lb)

- Pumpkin puree (1 can)

- Black beans (1 can, drained and rinsed)

- Diced tomatoes (1 can)

- Onion (1, diced)

- Garlic (2 cloves, minced)

- Chili powder (2 tbsp)

- Cumin (1 tbsp, ground)

- Salt and pepper to taste

Preparation:

- Brown ground turkey in a pan, then transfer to the slow cooker.

- Add pumpkin puree, black beans, diced tomatoes, onion, garlic, chili powder, cumin, salt, and pepper.
- Cook on low for 4-5 hours.

Nutritional values per serving:

- Protein: 25g
- Fat: 8g
- Carbohydrates: 30g
- Calories: 270

Serves: 4

Ingredients:

- Stewing beef (1 lb, cubed)

- Barley (1/2 cup, uncooked)

- Carrots (1 cup, sliced)

- Celery (1 cup, sliced)

- Low-sodium beef broth (4 cups)

- Onion (1, diced)

- Garlic (2 cloves, minced)

- Thyme (1 tsp, dried)

- Salt and pepper to taste

Preparation:

- Brown beef in a pan, then transfer to the slow cooker.

- Add barley, carrots, celery, beef broth, onion, garlic, thyme, salt, and pepper.

- Cook on low for 6-8 hours or high for 3-4 hours until beef is tender.

Nutritional values per serving:

- Protein: 25g

- Fat: 10g

- Carbohydrates: 30g

- Calories: 300

Serves: 3

Ingredients:

- Salmon fillets (3, skinless)

- Potatoes (2, thinly sliced)

- Onion (1, thinly sliced)

- Garlic (2 cloves, minced)

- Lemon juice (2 tbsp)

- Olive oil (2 tbsp)

- Dill (1 tsp, dried)

- Salt and pepper to taste

Preparation:

- Grease the slow cooker and layer potatoes, onion, and garlic.

- Season salmon with salt, pepper, dill, lemon juice, and olive oil. Place on top of the potatoes.
- Cook on low for 2-3 hours until salmon flakes easily and potatoes are tender.

Nutritional values per serving:

- Protein: 25g
- Fat: 10g
- Carbohydrates: 20g
- Calories: 260

Serves: 4

Ingredients:

- Eggs (6)
- Bell peppers (2, diced)
- Mushrooms (1 cup, sliced)
- Spinach (2 cups)
- Onion (1, diced)
- Garlic (2 cloves, minced)
- Cheese (1 cup, shredded)
- Salt and pepper to taste

Preparation:

- In a pan, sauté bell peppers, mushrooms, onion, and garlic until softened.

- Grease the slow cooker and layer sautéed vegetables, spinach, and cheese.
- Beat eggs with salt and pepper, then pour over the vegetables and cheese.
- Cook on low for 3-4 hours until set.

Nutritional values per serving:

- Protein: 15g
- Fat: 12g
- Carbohydrates: 10g
- Calories: 200

Serves: 4

Ingredients:

- Chicken thighs (1 lb, boneless and skinless, diced)
- Arborio rice (1 cup)
- Chicken broth (2 cups)
- Peas (1 cup)
- Onion (1, diced)
- Garlic (2 cloves, minced)
- Parmesan cheese (1/2 cup, grated)
- Salt and pepper to taste

Preparation:

- Brown chicken in a pan, then transfer to the slow cooker.

- Add Arborio rice, chicken broth, peas, onion, garlic, salt, and pepper.

- Cook on low for 6-8 hours or high for 3-4 hours until rice is creamy and chicken is cooked through.

- Stir in Parmesan cheese before serving.

Nutritional values per serving:

- Protein: 30g

- Fat: 12g

- Carbohydrates: 30g

- Calories: 320

Serves: 4

Ingredients:

- Ground turkey (1 lb)
- Whole wheat pasta (8 oz, cooked)
- Marinara sauce (2 cups)
- Onion (1, diced)
- Garlic (2 cloves, minced)
- Italian seasoning (1 tbsp)
- Parmesan cheese (1/4 cup, grated)
- Salt and pepper to taste

Preparation:

- In a bowl, combine ground turkey, onion, garlic, Italian seasoning, salt, and pepper. Form into meatballs.

- Brown meatballs in a pan, then transfer to the slow cooker.

- Add cooked pasta and marinara sauce.

- Cook on low for 4-5 hours until meatballs are cooked through.

- Sprinkle with Parmesan cheese before serving.

Nutritional values per serving:

- Protein: 25g

- Fat: 8g

- Carbohydrates: 30g

- Calories: 270

Serves: 6

Ingredients:

- Ground beef (1 lb)

- Lasagna noodles (8 oz, uncooked)

- Marinara sauce (2 cups)

- Ricotta cheese (1 cup)

- Spinach (2 cups)

- Mozzarella cheese (1 cup, shredded)

- Parmesan cheese (1/4 cup, grated)

- Italian seasoning (1 tbsp)

- Salt and pepper to taste

Preparation:

- Brown ground beef in a pan, then drain excess fat.

- In the slow cooker, layer marinara sauce, lasagna noodles, ricotta cheese, spinach, ground beef, mozzarella cheese, Parmesan cheese, Italian seasoning, salt, and pepper.

- Repeat layers as needed, ending with a layer of sauce and cheese on top.

- Cook on low for 4-5 hours until noodles are tender.

Nutritional values per serving:

- Protein: 30g

- Fat: 18g

- Carbohydrates: 15g

- Calories: 320

Serves: 3

Ingredients:

- Salmon fillets (3, skinless)
- Sweet potatoes (2, peeled and diced)
- Corn (1 cup)
- Celery (1 cup, sliced)
- Onion (1, diced)
- Low-sodium chicken broth (2 cups)
- Milk (1 cup)
- Garlic (2 cloves, minced)
- Dill (1 tsp, dried)
- Salt and pepper to taste

Preparation:

- Place salmon at the bottom of the slow cooker.

- Add sweet potatoes, corn, celery, onion, chicken broth, milk, garlic, dill, salt, and pepper.

- Cook on low for 2-3 hours until salmon flakes easily and sweet potatoes are tender.

Nutritional values per serving:

- Protein: 25g

- Fat: 8g

- Carbohydrates: 20g

- Calories: 260

Serves: 4

Ingredients:

- Eggs (8)
- Whole wheat English muffins (4)
- Cheese slices (4)
- Spinach (2 cups)
- Tomato slices (4)
- Salt and pepper to taste

Preparation:

- Beat eggs with salt and pepper.
- Grease the slow cooker and pour in beaten eggs.
- Cook on low for 2-3 hours until set.
- Assemble sandwiches with eggs, cheese, spinach, and tomato slices.

Nutritional values per serving:

- Protein: 15g

- Fat: 12g

- Carbohydrates: 20g

- Calories: 250

Chicken and Vegetable Stir-Fry

Serves: 4

Ingredients:

- Chicken breast (1 lb, boneless and skinless, thinly sliced)

- Broccoli florets (2 cups)

- Bell peppers (2, thinly sliced)

- Carrots (1 cup, thinly sliced)

- Snow peas (1 cup)

- Onion (1, thinly sliced)

- Garlic (2 cloves, minced)

- Soy sauce (1/4 cup)

- Honey (2 tbsp)

- Ginger (1 tbsp, minced)

- Olive oil (2 tbsp)

- Sesame seeds (1 tbsp, for garnish)

- Salt and pepper to taste

Preparation:

- In a bowl, mix soy sauce, honey, ginger, olive oil, salt, and pepper.

- Grease the slow cooker and layer chicken, broccoli, bell peppers, carrots, snow peas, onion, and garlic.

- Pour the sauce over the layers.

- Cook on low for 3-4 hours until chicken is cooked through and vegetables are tender.
- Garnish with sesame seeds before serving.

Nutritional values per serving:

- Protein: 25g
- Fat: 10g
- Carbohydrates: 30g
- Calories: 280

Serves: 3

Ingredients:

- Ground turkey (1 lb)

- Quinoa (1 cup, cooked)

- Cherry tomatoes (1 cup, halved)

- Cucumber (1, diced)

- Red onion (1/2, thinly sliced)

- Kalamata olives (1/4 cup, sliced)

- Feta cheese (1/2 cup, crumbled)

- Lemon juice (2 tbsp)

- Olive oil (2 tbsp)

- Oregano (1 tsp, dried)

- Salt and pepper to taste

Preparation:

- Brown ground turkey in a pan, then transfer to the slow cooker.

- In a bowl, combine cooked quinoa, cherry tomatoes, cucumber, red onion, Kalamata olives, feta cheese, lemon juice, olive oil, oregano, salt, and pepper.

- Serve ground turkey over the quinoa salad.

Nutritional values per serving:

- Protein: 25g

- Fat: 12g

- Carbohydrates: 20g

- Calories: 270

Serves: 6

Ingredients:

- Stewing beef (1 lb, cubed)

- Broccoli florets (3 cups)

- Brown rice (1 cup, uncooked)

- Low-sodium beef broth (2 cups)

- Onion (1, diced)

- Garlic (2 cloves, minced)

- Soy sauce (1/4 cup)

- Cornstarch (2 tbsp, dissolved in water)

- Olive oil (2 tbsp)

- Sesame oil (1 tsp)

- Salt and pepper to taste

Preparation:

- Brown beef in a pan, then transfer to the slow cooker.

- Add broccoli, brown rice, beef broth, onion, garlic, soy sauce, salt, and pepper.

- Cook on low for 6-8 hours or high for 3-4 hours until beef is tender and rice is cooked.

- Stir in cornstarch mixture and sesame oil during the last 30 minutes of cooking to thicken the sauce.

Nutritional values per serving:

- Protein: 30g

- Fat: 18g

- Carbohydrates: 15g

- Calories: 320

DINNER

Chicken and Rice Casserole

Serves: 4

Ingredients:

- Chicken thighs (1 lb, boneless and skinless)

- White rice (1 cup, uncooked)

- Carrots (1 cup, sliced)

- Peas (1 cup)

- Low-sodium chicken broth (2 cups)

- Onion (1, diced)

- Garlic (2 cloves, minced)

- Thyme (1 tsp, dried)

- Salt and pepper to taste

Preparation:

- Place chicken thighs, white rice, carrots, peas, chicken broth, onion, garlic, thyme, salt, and pepper in the slow cooker.
- Cook on low for 6-8 hours or high for 3-4 hours until chicken is tender and rice is cooked.
- Shred the chicken before serving.

Nutritional values per serving:

- Protein: 30g
- Fat: 5g
- Carbohydrates: 40g
- Calories: 300

Serves: 3

Ingredients:

- Ground turkey (1 lb)

- Sweet potatoes (2, peeled and diced)

- Carrots (1 cup, sliced)

- Celery (1 cup, sliced)

- Low-sodium chicken broth (2 cups)

- Onion (1, diced)

- Garlic (2 cloves, minced)

- Sage (1 tsp, dried)

- Salt and pepper to taste

Preparation:

- Brown ground turkey in a pan, then transfer to the slow cooker.

- Add sweet potatoes, carrots, celery, onion, garlic, sage, salt, and pepper.

- Pour chicken broth over the ingredients.

- Cook on low for 4-5 hours until vegetables are tender.

Nutritional values per serving:

- Protein: 20g

- Fat: 8g

- Carbohydrates: 30g

- Calories: 270

Serves: 4

Ingredients:

- Stewing beef (1 lb, cubed)

- Potatoes (2, diced)

- Carrots (1 cup, sliced)

- Celery (1 cup, sliced)

- Green beans (1 cup, chopped)

- Low-sodium beef broth (2 cups)

- Onion (1, diced)

- Garlic (2 cloves, minced)

- Rosemary (1 tsp, dried)

- Salt and pepper to taste

Preparation:

- Brown stewing beef in a pan, then transfer to the slow cooker.

- Add potatoes, carrots, celery, green beans, onion, garlic, rosemary, salt, and pepper.

- Pour beef broth over the ingredients.

- Cook on low for 6-8 hours or high for 3-4 hours until beef is tender and vegetables are cooked.

Nutritional values per serving:

- Protein: 30g

- Fat: 10g

- Carbohydrates: 30g

- Calories: 320

Serves: 3

Ingredients:

- Salmon fillets (3, skinless)
- Brown rice (1 cup, uncooked)
- Carrots (1 cup, diced)
- Peas (1 cup)
- Low-sodium chicken broth (2 cups)
- Onion (1, diced)
- Garlic (2 cloves, minced)
- Lemon juice (2 tbsp)
- Dill (1 tsp, dried)
- Salt and pepper to taste

Preparation:

- Place salmon fillets, brown rice, carrots, peas, chicken broth, onion, garlic, lemon juice, dill, salt, and pepper in the slow cooker.

- Cook on low for 2-3 hours until salmon flakes easily and rice is cooked.

- Stir gently to mix before serving.

Nutritional values per serving:

- Protein: 25g

- Fat: 8g

- Carbohydrates: 35g

- Calories: 300

Serves: 6

Ingredients:

- Eggs (8)
- Milk (1 cup)
- Cheddar cheese (1 cup, shredded)
- Spinach (2 cups, chopped)
- Bell peppers (1, diced)
- Onion (1, diced)
- Garlic (2 cloves, minced)
- Salt and pepper to taste

Preparation:

- In a bowl, beat eggs with milk, salt, and pepper.
- Grease the slow cooker and layer spinach, bell peppers, onion, garlic, and cheese.

- Pour the egg mixture over the layers.

- Cook on low for 3-4 hours until set.

Nutritional values per serving:

- Protein: 15g

- Fat: 12g

- Carbohydrates: 8g

- Calories: 180

Serves: 4

Ingredients:

- Lamb leg meat (1 lb, cubed)
- Pearl barley (1/2 cup, uncooked)
- Carrots (1 cup, sliced)
- Celery (1 cup, sliced)
- Low-sodium beef broth (4 cups)
- Onion (1, diced)
- Garlic (2 cloves, minced)
- Rosemary (1 tsp, dried)
- Salt and pepper to taste

Preparation:

- Brown lamb meat in a pan, then transfer to the slow cooker.

- Add pearl barley, carrots, celery, beef broth, onion, garlic, rosemary, salt, and pepper.
- Cook on low for 6-8 hours or high for 3-4 hours until lamb is tender and barley is cooked.

Nutritional values per serving:

- Protein: 30g
- Fat: 12g
- Carbohydrates: 35g
- Calories: 320

Serves: 4

Ingredients:

- Pork loin (1 lb, cubed)

- Apples (2, diced)

- Onion (1, diced)

- Garlic (2 cloves, minced)

- Curry powder (2 tbsp)

- Coconut milk (1 can)

- Low-sodium chicken broth (1 cup)

- Olive oil (2 tbsp)

- Salt and pepper to taste

Preparation:

- Brown pork loin cubes in a pan with olive oil, then transfer to the slow cooker.

- Add apples, onion, garlic, curry powder, coconut milk, chicken broth, salt, and pepper.

- Cook on low for 6-8 hours or high for 3-4 hours until pork is tender and flavors are well combined.

Nutritional values per serving:

- Protein: 25g

- Fat: 15g

- Carbohydrates: 20g

- Calories: 350

Serves: 4

Ingredients:

- Chicken thighs (1 lb, boneless and skinless)
- Lentils (1 cup, rinsed)
- Carrots (1 cup, sliced)
- Celery (1 cup, sliced)
- Low-sodium chicken broth (3 cups)
- Onion (1, diced)
- Garlic (2 cloves, minced)
- Cumin (1 tsp, ground)
- Paprika (1 tsp)
- Salt and pepper to taste

Preparation:

- Place chicken thighs, lentils, carrots, celery, chicken broth, onion, garlic, cumin, paprika, salt, and pepper in the slow cooker.

- Cook on low for 6-8 hours or high for 3-4 hours until chicken is tender and lentils are cooked.

- Shred the chicken before serving.

Nutritional values per serving:

- Protein: 30g

- Fat: 5g

- Carbohydrates: 35g

- Calories: 280

Serves: 4

Ingredients:

- Ground turkey (1 lb)

- Pumpkin puree (1 cup)

- Black beans (1 can, drained and rinsed)

- Diced tomatoes (1 can)

- Onion (1, diced)

- Garlic (2 cloves, minced)

- Chili powder (2 tbsp)

- Cumin (1 tsp)

- Paprika (1 tsp)

- Salt and pepper to taste

Preparation:

- Brown ground turkey in a pan, then transfer to the slow cooker.
- Add pumpkin puree, black beans, diced tomatoes, onion, garlic, chili powder, cumin, paprika, salt, and pepper.
- Stir well to combine all ingredients.
- Cook on low for 6-8 hours or high for 3-4 hours until flavors meld together.

Nutritional values per serving:

- Protein: 25g
- Fat: 8g
- Carbohydrates: 30g
- Calories: 270

Serves: 4

Ingredients:

- Stewing beef (1 lb, cubed)

- Potatoes (2, diced)

- Carrots (1 cup, sliced)

- Onion (1, diced)

- Garlic (2 cloves, minced)

- Worcestershire sauce (2 tbsp)

- Olive oil (2 tbsp)

- Salt and pepper to taste

Preparation:

- Brown stewing beef in a pan with olive oil, then transfer to the slow cooker.

- Add potatoes, carrots, onion, garlic, Worcestershire sauce, salt, and pepper.

- Cook on low for 6-8 hours or high for 3-4 hours until beef is tender and potatoes are cooked.

- Mash lightly for a hash-like consistency before serving.

Nutritional values per serving:

- Protein: 30g

- Fat: 10g

- Carbohydrates: 25g

- Calories: 300

Serves: 3

Ingredients:

- Salmon fillets (3, skinless)
- Quinoa (1 cup, cooked)
- Asparagus (1 bunch, trimmed)
- Cherry tomatoes (1 cup, halved)
- Lemon juice (2 tbsp)
- Olive oil (2 tbsp)
- Dill (1 tsp, dried)
- Salt and pepper to taste

Preparation:

- Season salmon fillets with lemon juice, olive oil, dill, salt, and pepper.

- Place asparagus spears at the bottom of the slow cooker.

- Layer cooked quinoa and cherry tomatoes over the asparagus.

- Arrange seasoned salmon fillets on top.

- Cover and cook on low for 2-3 hours until salmon is cooked through and vegetables are tender.

Nutritional values per serving:

- Protein: 25g

- Fat: 12g

- Carbohydrates: 30g

- Calories: 280

Serves: 4

Ingredients:

- Eggs (8)
- Bell peppers (2, sliced)
- Broccoli florets (2 cups)
- Snow peas (1 cup)
- Onion (1, sliced)
- Garlic (2 cloves, minced)
- Soy sauce (2 tbsp)
- Olive oil (2 tbsp)
- Ginger (1 tsp, minced)
- Salt and pepper to taste

Preparation:

- In a pan, sauté bell peppers, broccoli, snow peas, onion, garlic, and ginger with olive oil until tender.

- In a bowl, beat eggs with soy sauce, salt, and pepper.

- Grease the slow cooker and pour in the egg mixture.

- Top with the sautéed vegetables.

- Cover and cook on low for 2-3 hours until eggs are set.

Nutritional values per serving:

- Protein: 15g

- Fat: 10g

- Carbohydrates: 10g

- Calories: 160

Serves: 4

Ingredients:

- Chicken breasts (1 lb, boneless and skinless)
- Arborio rice (1 cup, uncooked)
- Peas (1 cup)
- Low-sodium chicken broth (3 cups)
- White wine (1/2 cup)
- Onion (1, diced)
- Garlic (2 cloves, minced)
- Parmesan cheese (1/2 cup, grated)
- Olive oil (2 tbsp)
- Salt and pepper to taste

Preparation:

- Brown chicken breasts in a pan with olive oil, then transfer to the slow cooker.

- Add Arborio rice, peas, chicken broth, white wine, onion, garlic, salt, and pepper.

- Cook on low for 6-8 hours or high for 3-4 hours until chicken is cooked and rice is creamy.

- Stir in grated Parmesan cheese before serving.

Nutritional values per serving:

- Protein: 30g

- Fat: 10g

- Carbohydrates: 35g

- Calories: 320

Turkey Meatball Pasta

Serves: 4

Ingredients:

- Ground turkey (1 lb)

- Whole wheat pasta (8 oz, cooked)

- Marinara sauce (2 cups)

- Parmesan cheese (1/2 cup, grated)

- Bread crumbs (1/2 cup)

- Egg (1)

- Onion (1/2, diced)

- Garlic (2 cloves, minced)

- Olive oil (2 tbsp)

- Italian seasoning (1 tbsp)

- Salt and pepper to taste

Preparation:

- In a bowl, combine ground turkey, bread crumbs, egg, onion, garlic, Italian seasoning, salt, and pepper. Form into meatballs.

- Brown meatballs in a pan with olive oil, then transfer to the slow cooker.

- Pour marinara sauce over the meatballs.

- Cook on low for 4-5 hours.

- Serve meatballs and sauce over cooked whole wheat pasta, garnished with grated Parmesan cheese.

Nutritional values per serving:

- Protein: 25g

- Fat: 10g

- Carbohydrates: 35g

- Calories: 320

Serves: 6

Ingredients:

- Ground beef (1 lb)

- Lasagna noodles (8 oz, cooked)

- Marinara sauce (2 cups)

- Ricotta cheese (1 cup)

- Mozzarella cheese (1 cup, shredded)

- Spinach (2 cups, chopped)

- Onion (1, diced)

- Garlic (2 cloves, minced)

- Olive oil (2 tbsp)

- Italian seasoning (1 tbsp)

- Salt and pepper to taste

Preparation:

- In a pan, cook ground beef with onion, garlic, Italian seasoning, salt, and pepper until browned.

- Grease the slow cooker and layer cooked lasagna noodles, beef mixture, marinara sauce, ricotta cheese, mozzarella cheese, and spinach.

- Repeat layers as needed, ending with a layer of cheese on top.

- Cook on low for 4-5 hours until lasagna is cooked through and cheese is melted and bubbly.

Nutritional values per serving:

- Protein: 30g
- Fat: 15g
- Carbohydrates: 40g
- Calories: 400

Serves: 3

Ingredients:

- Salmon fillets (3, skinless)

- Sweet potatoes (2, diced)

- Carrots (1 cup, sliced)

- Celery (1 cup, sliced)

- Low-sodium chicken broth (2 cups)

- Milk (1 cup)

- Onion (1, diced)

- Garlic (2 cloves, minced)

- Dill (1 tsp, dried)

- Salt and pepper to taste

Preparation:

- Place salmon fillets, sweet potatoes, carrots, celery, chicken broth, milk, onion, garlic, dill, salt, and pepper in the slow cooker.

- Cook on low for 2-3 hours until salmon flakes easily and vegetables are tender.

- Stir in milk and dill just before serving.

Nutritional values per serving:

- Protein: 25g

- Fat: 8g

- Carbohydrates: 20g

- Calories: 260

Serves: 4

Ingredients:

- Eggs (8)
- Cheddar cheese (1 cup, shredded)
- Spinach (2 cups, chopped)
- Onion (1, diced)
- Bell peppers (1, diced)
- Mushrooms (1 cup, sliced)
- Olive oil (2 tbsp)
- Salt and pepper to taste

Preparation:

- In a pan, sauté onion, bell peppers, mushrooms, and spinach with olive oil until tender.
- In a bowl, beat eggs with salt and pepper.

- Grease the slow cooker and pour in the egg mixture.

- Top with sautéed vegetables and shredded cheese.

- Cook on low for 2-3 hours until eggs are set and cheese is melted.

Nutritional values per serving:

- Protein: 15g

- Fat: 12g

- Carbohydrates: 8g

- Calories: 180

Serves: 6

Ingredients:

- Chicken breasts (1 lb, boneless and skinless)
- Potatoes (2, diced)
- Carrots (1 cup, sliced)
- Green beans (2 cups, chopped)
- Low-sodium chicken broth (2 cups)
- Onion (1, diced)
- Garlic (2 cloves, minced)
- Italian seasoning (1 tbsp)
- Olive oil (2 tbsp)
- Salt and pepper to taste

Preparation:

- Brown chicken breasts in a pan with olive oil, then transfer to the slow cooker.

- Add potatoes, carrots, green beans, onion, garlic, Italian seasoning, salt, and pepper.

- Pour chicken broth over the ingredients.

- Cook on low for 6-8 hours or high for 3-4 hours until chicken is cooked through and vegetables are tender.

Nutritional values per serving:

- Protein: 30g

- Fat: 8g

- Carbohydrates: 30g

- Calories: 280

Serves: 4

Ingredients:

- Ground turkey (1 lb)

- Quinoa (1 cup, cooked)

- Cucumber (1, diced)

- Cherry tomatoes (1 cup, halved)

- Red onion (1/2, diced)

- Feta cheese (1/2 cup, crumbled)

- Olive oil (2 tbsp)

- Lemon juice (2 tbsp)

- Fresh parsley (2 tbsp, chopped)

- Salt and pepper to taste

Preparation:

Brown ground turkey in a pan with olive oil, then let it cool.

- In a large bowl, combine cooked quinoa, cucumber, cherry tomatoes, red onion, feta cheese, and cooled ground turkey.
- Drizzle with olive oil and lemon juice, then add chopped parsley, salt, and pepper. Toss to combine.
- Serve chilled or at room temperature.

Nutritional values per serving:

- Protein: 20g
- Fat: 10g
- Carbohydrates: 25g
- Calories: 250

Serves: 4

Ingredients:

- Beef sirloin (1 lb, thinly sliced)

- Broccoli florets (2 cups)

- Bell peppers (2, sliced)

- Onion (1, sliced)

- Garlic (2 cloves, minced)

- Soy sauce (2 tbsp)

- Honey (1 tbsp)

- Olive oil (2 tbsp)

- Cornstarch (1 tbsp)

- Water (1/4 cup)

- Sesame seeds (1 tbsp, optional for garnish)

- Salt and pepper to taste

Preparation:

- In a bowl, whisk together soy sauce, honey, cornstarch, water, salt, and pepper to make the sauce.
- Brown beef slices in a pan with olive oil, then transfer to the slow cooker.
- Add broccoli, bell peppers, onion, and garlic to the slow cooker.
- Pour the sauce over the ingredients.
- Cook on low for 2-3 hours until beef is cooked and vegetables are tender.
- Garnish with sesame seeds before serving if desired.

Nutritional values per serving:

- Protein: 25g
- Fat: 10g
- Carbohydrates: 20g
- Calories: 280

MEAL PLAN

Day 1

- **Breakfast**: Chicken and Broccoli Casserole
- **Lunch**: Turkey and Pumpkin Chili
- **Dinner**: Beef and Vegetable Stew

Day 2

- **Breakfast**: Egg and Cheese Breakfast Burritos
- **Lunch**: Beef and Barley Stew
- **Dinner**: Salmon and Quinoa Bake

Day 3

- **Breakfast**: Salmon and Pea Frittata
- **Lunch**: Egg and Veggie Scramble

* **Dinner**: Chicken and Vegetable Casserole

Day 4

* **Breakfast**: Turkey and Pumpkin Breakfast Casserole
* **Lunch**: Turkey Meatball Pasta
* **Dinner**: Beef and Broccoli Stir-Fry

Day 5

* **Breakfast**: Lamb and Rice Medley
* **Lunch**: Chicken and Pea Risotto
* **Dinner**: Salmon and Sweet Potato Chowder

Day 6

* **Breakfast**: Beef and Spinach Hash
* **Lunch**: Salmon and Potato Bake

- **Dinner**: Turkey and Sweet Potato Stew

Day 7

- **Breakfast**: Pork and Apple Oatmeal
- **Lunch**: Egg and Cheese Casserole
- **Dinner**: Beef and Potato Hash

Day 8

- **Breakfast**: Chicken and Sweet Potato Stew
- **Lunch**: Lamb and Brown Rice Pilaf
- **Dinner**: Turkey and Quinoa Salad

Day 9

- **Breakfast**: Turkey Bacon Breakfast Soup
- **Lunch**: Pork and Apple Stew
- **Dinner**: Chicken and Lentil Stew

Day 10

- **Breakfast**: Egg and Veggie Casserole
- **Lunch**: Chicken and Rice Soup
- **Dinner**: Salmon and Brown Rice Pilaf

Day 11

- **Breakfast**: Beef and Barley Breakfast Soup
- **Lunch**: Beef and Spinach Lasagna
- **Dinner**: Egg and Cheese Quiche

Day 12

- **Breakfast**: Turkey Sausage Breakfast Bowl
- **Lunch**: Salmon and Quinoa Salad
- **Dinner**: Turkey and Pumpkin Chili

Day 13

- **Breakfast**: Salmon and Potato Chowder
- **Lunch**: Chicken and Lentil Curry
- **Dinner**: Beef and Vegetable Stew

Day 14

- **Breakfast**: Turkey and Veggie Stuffed Peppers
- **Lunch**: Egg and Cheese Sandwiches
- **Dinner**: Chicken and Rice Casserole

MEAL PLANNER

SLOW COOKER
COOKBOOK FOR
LABRADOR
RETRIEVERS

Weekly

WEEK ________________ MONTH ________________

MONDAY

SATURDAY

TUESDAY

SUNDAY

WEDNESDAY

SHOPPING LIST

THURSDAY

FRIDAY

SLOW COOKER COOKBOOK FOR LABRADOR RETRIEVERS

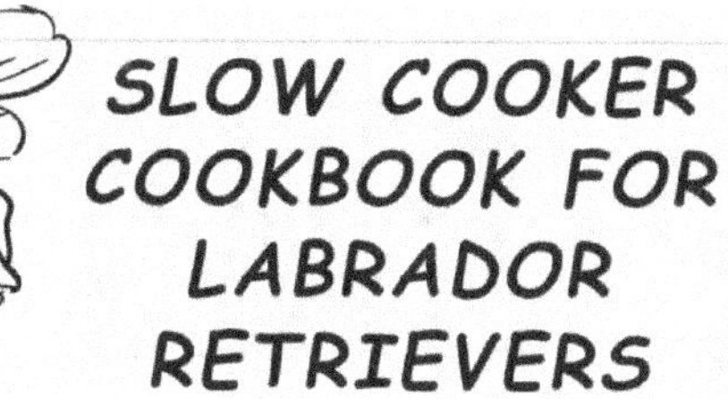

WEEK ___________   MONTH ___________

MONDAY

SATURDAY

TUESDAY

SUNDAY

WEDNESDAY

SHOPPING LIST

THURSDAY

FRIDAY

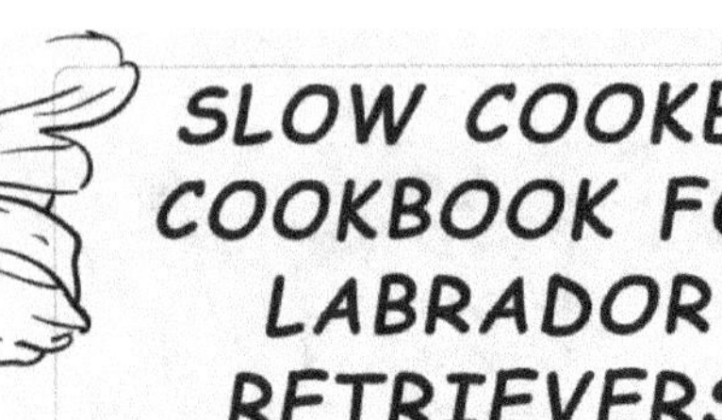

WEEK ___________________

MONTH ___________________

MONDAY

TUESDAY

WEDNESDAY

THURSDAY

FRIDAY

SATURDAY

SUNDAY

SHOPPING LIST

SLOW COOKER COOKBOOK FOR LABRADOR RETRIEVERS

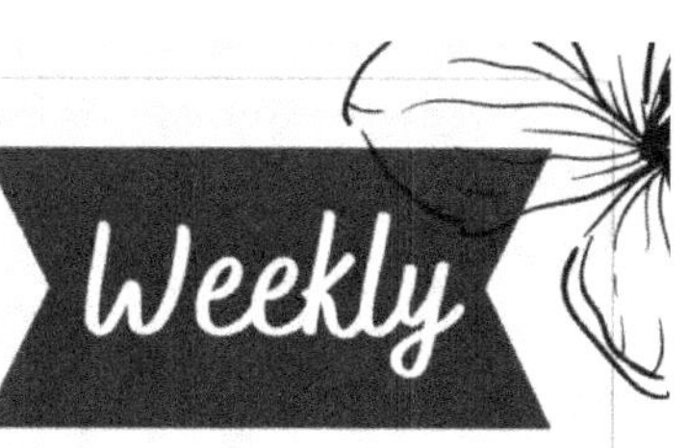

Weekly

WEEK ____________ MONTH ____________

MONDAY

TUESDAY

WEDNESDAY

THURSDAY

FRIDAY

SATURDAY

SUNDAY

SHOPPING LIST

- ○ ____________
- ○ ____________
- ○ ____________
- ○ ____________
- ○ ____________
- ○ ____________
- ○ ____________
- ○ ____________
- ○ ____________
- ○ ____________
- ○ ____________
- ○ ____________
- ○ ____________

SLOW COOKER COOKBOOK FOR LABRADOR RETRIEVERS

Weekly

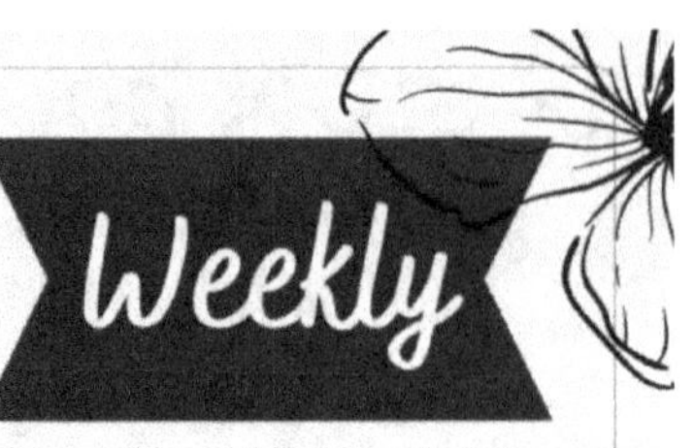

WEEK ______________ MONTH ______________

MONDAY

TUESDAY

WEDNESDAY

THURSDAY

FRIDAY

SATURDAY

SUNDAY

SHOPPING LIST

- ○ ______________
- ○ ______________
- ○ ______________
- ○ ______________
- ○ ______________
- ○ ______________
- ○ ______________
- ○ ______________
- ○ ______________
- ○ ______________
- ○ ______________
- ○ ______________
- ○ ______________

WEEK ____________________   MONTH ____________________

MONDAY

TUESDAY

WEDNESDAY

THURSDAY

FRIDAY

SATURDAY

SUNDAY

SHOPPING LIST

WEEK _______________   MONTH _______________

MONDAY

SATURDAY

TUESDAY

SUNDAY

WEDNESDAY

SHOPPING LIST

THURSDAY

FRIDAY

WEEK ____________________   MONTH ____________________

MONDAY	SATURDAY

TUESDAY	SUNDAY

WEDNESDAY

THURSDAY

FRIDAY

SHOPPING LIST

CONCLUSION

For those about to embark on preparing the recipes in this Slow Cooker Cookbook for Labrador Retrievers, get ready for a delightful journey filled with wagging tails, happy barks, and healthy meals that will nourish your furry friend from nose to tail.

Embrace the convenience of the slow cooker and savor the joy of creating homemade goodness that brings both you and your Labrador closer together.

And for those who have already experienced the magic of this cookbook, pat yourselves on the back for providing your Labrador with the love and care they deserve.

Your dedication to their well-being shines through in every nutritious meal, and the smiles and tail wags they give in return are a testament to the special bond you share.

Whether you're just starting or have become a seasoned chef for your Labrador, remember that every meal prepared with love is a celebration of the unbreakable bond between humans and their loyal companions.

Here's to many more happy meals and wagging tails in the days to come!

GAIN ACCESS TO MORE BOOKS FROM THIS AUTHOR